First World War
and Army of Occupation
War Diary
France, Belgium and Germany

59 DIVISION
177 Infantry Brigade
Lincolnshire Regiment
2/4 Battalion
4 January 1916 - 29 February 1916

WO95/3023/1

The Naval & Military Press Ltd
www.nmarchive.com
Published in association with The National Archives

Published by

The Naval & Military Press Ltd

Unit 10 Ridgewood Industrial Park,

Uckfield, East Sussex,

TN22 5QE England

Tel: +44 (0) 1825 749494

www.naval-military-press.com

www.nmarchive.com

This diary has been reprinted in facsimile from the original. Any imperfections are inevitably reproduced and the quality may fall short of modern type and cartographic standards.

© Crown Copyright
Images reproduced by permission of The National Archives, London, England, 2015.

Contents

Document type	Place/Title	Date From	Date To
Heading	59th Division 177th Infy Bde 2-4th Bn Lincoln Regt Feb 1917-1918 Jan And 1916 Jan Feb		
Heading	WO95/3023/1 2/4 Battalion Lincolnshire Regiment		
Heading	War Diary Of 2/4 Lincolnshire Regiment From January 1st 1916 To January 31st-1916		
War Diary	Harpenden	04/01/1916	31/01/1916
Heading	War Diary Of The 2/4 Bn. Lincolnshire Regiment From 1st. February 1916 To 29th. February 1916		
War Diary	Harpenden	01/02/1916	29/02/1916

59TH DIVISION
177TH INFY BDE

2-4TH BN LINCOLN REGT
FEB 1917 — 1918 JAN

AND

1916 JAN & FEB

Amalgamated with

4 LINCS FEB 1918

IN 39 DIV 118 B..

3023

WO95/3023/1
2/4 Battalion Lincolnshire Regiment

177/59 59 DIV
       177 BDE   (8)

Confidential

War Diary

of

2/4 Lincolnshire Regiment

From Jany 1st 1916   to Jany 31st 1916

A. Hitchins
Lt Col.
2/4 Lincolnshire Rgt

2/4 Lincolns.

WAR DIARY
or
INTELLIGENCE SUMMARY.
(Erase heading not required.)

Army Form C. 2118.

HEADQUARTERS
No. S/1/0/.
8 - FEB 1916
177th INFANTRY BRIGADE

Hour, Date, Place	Summary of Events and Information	Remarks and references to Appendices
	Except on days specified nothing of importance occurred & ordinary Routine training was carried out.	
4.1.16. HARPENDEN.	Brig Gen eq Blackader D.S.O. arrived & assumed command of this (177th) Infy Brigade, vice Col G. M. Jackson.	W.H.P.
6.1.16. HARPENDEN.	"A" & "B" Companies begun Special Company Training.	W.H.P.
22.1.16. HARPENDEN.	Arrival of first batch of Recruits from Army Reserve Class B (Ford Derby's Scheme) Detail of arrivals as under:— 20.1.1.16. 38 ; 24.1.16. 42 ; 26.1.16. 58. 27.1.16. 46. 25.1.16. 55. Total 269.	W.H.P.
26.1.16. HARPENDEN.	100 Short Rifles complete with Bayonets etc. arrived. Primarily for use on Range.	W.H.P.
27.1.16. HARPENDEN.	Re-Adjustment of Billet Areas of Units & Companies completed to meet exigencies of arrivals of new Recruits.	W.H.P.
31.1.16. HARPENDEN.	Alarm of Zeppelin Raid. Aerial Guard warned and posted. Nothing seen, though it is believed that hostile aircraft were in the vicinity.	W.H.P.

A. Stater
Lt Col
2/4 Lincolnshire Regt

CONFIDENTIAL

WAR   DIARY

of

The 2/4 Bn. Lincolnshire Regiment.

from 1st. February 1916 to 29th. February 1916.

(Page 8)

Army Form C. 2118.

WAR DIARY
or
INTELLIGENCE SUMMARY.
(Erase heading not required.)

Instructions regarding War Diaries and Intelligence Summaries are contained in F.S. Regs., Part II. and the Staff Manual respectively. Title pages will be prepared in manuscript.

Hour, Date, Place	Summary of Events and Information	Remarks and references to Appendices
1-2-16 HARPENDEN	Every day, except [illegible] of [illegible] [illegible] in [illegible] [illegible] Return training was carried out	
3-6-16 HARPENDEN	Inspection (in [illegible] of Battn) by Major Genl. heads of REDMOND by first line (for the A.S. inspection) K.R. & O.C.A. Commanding [illegible] Army General [illegible] A.T. & M.G. completed Special Training	
7-13-16 HARPENDEN	Programme of [illegible] extensive [illegible] defence & [illegible] of [illegible] to Bttn training was carried out	
14-2-16 HARPENDEN	Major Genl. A.E. SANDBACH C.B. D.S.O. The General of the Division inspected & gave from R.M.R. Booth Bn. to be inspected & take up another appointment	
21-2-16 HARPENDEN	Bn. per 1st Riflis [illegible] HARPENDEN (OFFICERS' Parade paraded marched to [illegible] and [illegible] the Payne visited some of 7.20 am 70 men injured parties in the LEICESTERS area	
29.2.16 HARPENDEN	[illegible] transport [illegible] BATT. paraded 6 pm ready & march off & S.O. Sergeants about [illegible] & 8.15 pm [illegible] to [illegible] in BDN magazine Reserve	

[signature]
Commanding 2/4 Lein. Regt.

www.ingramcontent.com/pod-product-compliance
Lightning Source LLC
Chambersburg PA
CBHW081516160426
43193CB00014B/2707